EVE'S THOUGHTS AND REFLECTIONS

Eve Theresa Marie Carter

authorHOUSE®

AuthorHouse™
1663 Liberty Drive
Bloomington, IN 47403
www.authorhouse.com
Phone: 1 (800) 839-8640

Published by AuthorHouse 03/18/2016

ISBN: 978-1-5049-7973-3 (sc)
ISBN: 978-1-5049-7972-6 (e)

Print information available on the last page.

Any people depicted in stock imagery provided by Thinkstock are models,
and such images are being used for illustrative purposes only.
Certain stock imagery © Thinkstock.

This book is printed on acid-free paper.

Because of the dynamic nature of the Internet, any web addresses or
links contained in this book may have changed since publication and
may no longer be valid. The views expressed in this work are solely those
of the author and do not necessarily reflect the views of the publisher,
and the publisher hereby disclaims any responsibility for them.

*This book is dedicated to my
very beautiful daughter:
Sandra Theresa Piercy. She has three very beautiful
girls which I dearly and truly love from the depth
of my heart.*

GARNET

January's Child

One look at you the angels
and God knew that you
were heaven sent and been
blessed with a magical moment
which hovered above you
when you were lovingly
placed in your mothers
warm arms of love's pure kiss.

~ ~ ~

You're my January's child
Born on the 10th a
Sacred stone of
Garnet
You're my
Dearest prized
Jewel.

~ ~ ~

1

Eve Theresa Marie Carter

In this favorable month
there are so many distinctive
qualities known for this creative
energy of garnet stone. This stone has been
around since the middle ages. In
ancient Greek and Roman times, according to
Talmud the only light on Noah's ark was
provided by the precious largestone of Garnet.
This stone enhances faith, constancy melancholy
and truth. Also was derived from the
Latin name Granatum, which resonates a
variety of bearing the seeds of a pomegranate.

~ ~ ~

May you forever be blessed upon
every grain of grass, sand and earthen
décor as never straying from your beauty
and beloved nature as you walk in the grace
of everything you touch, smell and lovingly adore.

~ ~ ~

January's flower is the Carnation which its
general meaning is filled with
fascination, distinction and love
within their hearts. In the earliest
times this floral flower was
known throughout the Roman Empire days.
The person who is born in this
month does portray a stable,

trustworthy persona, are ambitious
and are known to
be persistant in all endeavors they do.

On Jan. 1

You are a timeless
Fresh breath of precious skilled art

On Jan 2

On the day that you were born
we were blessed with the purity
of having you;
has kept me in awe
with the
beauty of you.

Jan. 3

With this thought in mind
God and the angels

Are watching and guiding
You to your chosen path.

Jan. 4

Your honesty, your passion
Your beautiful smile
Makes my day,
So please make every moment
count and good things will
surely be offered to you.
You remind me as if
YOU'RE
like an eternal flame
which is transparent
throughout your beauty of face.

Jan 5

My friend,
My daughter
Your beauty is
Beyond compare,
let no man belittle you
for you are a beauty far
beyond your beautiful heart.

Jan. 6

In every walk and breath in a persons life
A new horizon will be offered
to you with each and every passing
of day and night.

Jan. 7

When contemplating an unknown barrier
make the most of any given situation.
Measure everything with
an equal balance
Then you'll be rewarded with
life's most meaningful treasure.

Jan. 8

The power of love
A mother has
Is transferred to
Her adult children.
Then after she will always
know that she has brought them
up with every moment of everlasting
love and heartfelt devotion.

Jan. 9

Throughout every woman or
mans life, there will always
be an unknown force within
themselves. To let their voices
be heard. Then their life will be
well balanced with sincerity of
an honest days work and
a meaningful life.

On Jan. 10

On this day that you were born
I was given the best of a
beautiful child, a beauty beyond
any words could ever explain.
To me you were the best thing
that has ever happened to me.
One look in your little eyes,
I initially thought you were
like a mystical stone
like that precious
stone of a garnet
sparkling like
a fiery stone
held up high
in the sky like

a glowing
shooting star.

~ ~ ~

God had given me
The best gift of all
My dearest treasured child
My beautiful loving
Daughter

~ ~

Jan. 11

In the early times
of your mothers young
and earnest life, she will
always adore you for the woman
or man which you'll become
a steadfast individual with an earnest
and honest soul and you'll be enriched
with all that life has to offer you with
the precious most endearing love of your parents
forever more. We'll always cherish you with
all our love in each passing day,
year and months ahead.

~ ~ ~

Jan. 12

Count your blessings; God is love
You'll be granted his divinity of power

Jan. 13

Pray and the Lord prays with you
Let him walk you through his salvation of land.
Keep him near and you'll be measured beyond,
your great expectations of being a firm believer
in every thing you say, do, and walk on
with an open and intelligent well-defined mind.

Jan. 14

Shine through with his warmth of truth
And you'll become a pure divine woman of
A true and magnificent Garnet of Stone

Jan. 15

Sing praises of love through each and everyday
Then you'll have a great vast amount of knowledge
so beyond your youthful young years ahead.

Jan. 16

You'll be rewarded in God's loving arms,
therefore you'll be enraptured
of all his beautiful charms.

Jan. 17

Love yourself then others will love you
With all honesty of pure of heartfelt
tears of joy throughout many years ahead.

Jan. 18

Knowing who and why you're beauty is quite rare.
Your beauty surely shines like the brightest star.

~ ~ ~

Jan. 19

Courage takes a great tremendous
of positive attitude.
With strength comes an eternal life
of a meaningful journey.

~ ~ ~

Jan. 20

Know your beliefs well,
then make a justifiable statement
Of attitude, reliance and note-worthy
thoughts knowing your self- worth
Can be the best thing in your life.

~ ~ ~

Jan. 21

Let there be so many happy tunes
for this is the first month of a new
and vibrant year. Let all the love of
your beautiful children adore you for
Your great passion and zeal for life,
is waiting for you to enhance their

startling minds and hearts to reach
far beyond their young life's ahead.

Jan. 22

I asked the Lord to comfort me
In all his treasured moments each day.

Jan. 23

Along the way the Lord had to say
Be strong in mind, then you'll
be rewarded with the gift of life.

Jan. 24

In life's greatest journey so far;
You're my biggest inspiration
and love in my heart.

Jan. 25

The Lord had blessed me with thee
I've walked this life with true happiness, of
knowing you're my best friend.

Jan. 26

Now I feel some content today
For your divine guidance has kept me to
Be a true down to earth kind of gal.
Just knowing you're in my life
makes every grain of essence like
a fine cup of fresh air within all
your fine exquisite finesse in all that you do.

Jan. 27

Eventually my legs will walk under stars,
Like the true beauty within your magical eyes.

Jan. 28

I asked the Lord to comfort me
While he graced me with your youth.

Jan. 29

He gave me a reason to live graciously
In his loving devotional inviting arms.

Jan. 30

In longevity's serenity,
I found my destiny
When I set my eyes on you.
I always remember all the beauty
of holding you in my beloved arms.

Jan. 31

The stars are shining brightly
upon everyone tonight for they're
Sparkling like diamonds in the sky.

~ ~ ~

AMETHYST

February's Child

Bringing and singing will bring radiance
And the beauty of a smile
While embracing the power
Of love like the lightened
Color of lilac hue.
Long may you
Embellish lives
Symbolic of
Health, hope and love
Then within your
Beauty of
Youth.
You'll reach
out to all matters
within your intelligent
heart and soul.

February's Child

Is enriched with Amethyst's gold
Throughout history, this stone
has great healing powers.
It's quite the most precious gift
of all. To be held in the
greatest thoughts through- out all
time. This stone has the
greatest depth of vibrant colors, as like lilac
hues to the darkest exotic of purple rays.

If you were born into this favorable month
know that you have the all elusive scent of the floral
violets which means that true
love does exist. Just know
that in this month some people
have been known that they
may be of quiet of nature and have
some form of Latin in them
which signifies in latin terms means
a form of purification.

Feb. 1

In every walk and journey along the way
every step and breath has brought forth
the true meaning of our times well-spent.

Knowing that your my best friend will be
forever embedded in my heart and mind.

Feb. 2

With every opportunity in moderation
A thinking and knowledgeable mannered-man
Can learn a great deal from their spouses intellectual
earnest and kind well spoken
words per say. Will always
be in my devoted and eager mind
forever until the end of time.

Feb. 3

In life's greatest journey so thus far
You'll be walking a well- lighted path.
With fortitude and certain truthfulness
Your devotional heart will be blessed with purity.

Feb. 4

Till you walk with all the Lords words of passionate
vows you'll be tenderly loved within his heart

every day into his loving embrace.
Let it be known that we'll both be forever
and deeply well-defined and will always
be forever special kindred friends.

Feb. 5

The Lord had brought an insurmountable
Of knowledge so wise he also
gave you God's graceful loving eyes.
With all his glorifed loving heart
you'll always be measured with
a beautiful heart and know that he loves all.

Feb. 6

For in this treasured peacefulness per say
Your well educated mind will come a long way.

Feb. 7

Under your heavenly skies tonight, the greatest
gift is knowing you shine brighter than the stars.

Feb. 8

Be kind to your neighbors and close to
your peers, then you'll walk with an
honest days worth to know that you give off
the radiance of perception that your life will
intensify when you have a positive attitude
in every thing you say and do.

Feb. 9

You are my flaming star; like the all allusive
Comet that dances so fast upon the darkest night.

~ ~ ~

Feb. 10

I believe that anyone can make a difference
in life, if they gave more of themselves
to any given situation when they meet at hand.
Then they will be known as a true foundation
of knowing that they are so very well loved.

Feb. 11

Knowledge can be the great stepping stone
in life; utilize this and become an incurable
romantic soul as you walk
towards your eternal goal.

Feb. 12

On Earth, sing praises to one and all
Then let others know your intelligence.
For believing in what life has given you
A loving mother and father in all your young
loving hearts and souls in life's greatest long
journeys along with every step you take in time.

Feb 13

And onto this beautiful time of year
Brought forth a beautiful child
Well worth waiting for
For you'll always be wrapped
Around your loving parents
Arms forever in each and every passing day.
Our precious jewel which we all adorn is
Yours to have and to hold for all depth of time.

Feb. 14

Thus is our habitat for eternity so divine
For upon this day St. Valentine brought forth the
Sweetest joys of love is in your heart.

~ ~ ~

For unto many centuries love has
Been the strongest story ever for told
to which everyone's young or old lives.
Is finding the most precious gift of all
True Love lives on in all loving
Eyes!!

Feb. 15

The angels are telling you dear;
while they sing a heavenly tune, you'll always
be enveloped with warmth in your heart.
For the angels are always watching over you
with tenderness and love in their eyes.

Feb. 16

You made the right choice,
Let everyone hear your voice.

Then you'll have the greatest gift of all
An understanding true honest of heart.

Feb. 17

Remember to stay positive
With the messages you receive.
Then you'll be perceived with
the utmost challenge in your enchanted
realm of longevity's rule.

~ ~ ~

Feb. 18

A new beginning will come
and a new dawning will soon be one.
With this thought we'll all be united as a clear
and broadened mind and soul.

Feb. 19

For unto many centuries of so long ago
the falling stars had entered upon this earth's land.

For all the people on earth shall
be known as a kindred
kind of autumnal breeze within
your beauty of mind.

Feb. 20

In a new- land of tranquility there will be
a real gifted individual with great nobility.
Is knowing that you are waiting for me to share.

Feb. 21

Showers of love can bring happiness
and joy to us upon this eve,
Of an honest day's work and a wealth
of knowing you'll be wise.

Feb. 22

So we could have all fond memories to receive
Then you'll be rewarded with
grace of habitual thoughts.

Feb. 23

We hear many angels singing on this beauty of earth
As they are flowing and flying in
all lands of so far away.
They seem to be flaunting their wings
in tunes of great creativity
Which may enhance the bluest of
skies like an illusion of painting
the skies with all things magical
within your seeing eyes.

Feb. 24

Praise be to all for the lord gave us Great Tidings
and new beginning to be seen by one and all.

~ ~ ~

Feb. 25

A rippling effect
Crosses illusions sweetly
On petals of pearls
And lazily dances
Upon thin waters

Upon all hearts
A glow.

Feb. 26

Standing so close with
Graceful eyes brings beauty in
Your loving hearts true

Feb, 27

Let it be brought forward of
A new birth of a son Joe
A true beauty one.
In all your life you'll be
Walking into the strength
Of knowing that you were
Once a precious gift of life
As you lay in the beauty of
Your loving moms arms.

Feb. 28

Believe and the world
Will believe in you.

Note that the on the 29th is a saying
(quote) for the leap year
This is the day of my late beloved
grand-father's birthday
Alfred P. Whiteford

In ancient Egyptian times, they were the one's whom
decided of adding an extra day
once every four years.
To keep up in keeping the calendar
in sync. Then later
there after the Romans thus
adopted the solution that
they would initiate the first designated February 29
as the leap year.

Feb. 29

Throughout all mankind
You were given the greatest
Gift of all, on this day the ancients
Had befallen you the divine power
Of influencing your future son's

Your greatest gift of all
The blessings of the
Egyptians and Romans.

Your well skilled hands will bring forth
a son to be forever faithful of all your
Teachings and beliefs.

~ ~ ~

When you arrived on this precious
Momentous day all the Egyptians stood
Up and granted on having another day
Forth to celebrate that it takes the earth
Roughly 11 minutes and 14 seconds less than
365 ¼ days which means that each calendar
year may be over-shooting into the solar calendar.
A bit off by 11 minutes and 14 seconds per year.
On this very day brought forth
An extra days' worth of longevity's rule;
It will take about 1,095 more days to instill
another ones birthday to arrive again.
Unless they celebrate on March 1 or February 28.

~ ~ ~

BLOODSTONE

March's Child

May you long reign to give?
The greatest gift of all.

May you spread the seeds?
That blemish the soil
You walk on.

~ ~ ~

Another flower of March's view
Is the Jonquil, a narcissus with
Small clusters of yellow fragrant hues
Has been originated among the Latins
In the 17th century, also meaning rush reed.

~ ~ ~

Also in March thus marks
A plethora of dates devoted
To all mothers.

~ ~ ~

A Celtic Goddess is filtered within
the gift as in dear thought
Of sacred wells and of stills like
all calming flowing water.

~ ~ ~

She represents natural cycles of life.
In all concepts she brings forth
The many flowers and symbol of spring.

~ ~ ~

In ancient times of the Celts, honoring Coventina
They tossed sacred items in various bodies of water.
Such as brooches, coins and personal items.

March 1

May you be forever able to conceive
This big, big world does
Believe in all of the powers within you.

~ ~ ~

Thus for all the beloved on which this
day brought forth a beautiful
child into its sweet mother's arms.

~ ~ ~

March 2

God is protecting
All living things.
As he walks and is viewing
all living things in his
path to be known as the power of love.

March 3

He who walks alone
must keep a firm upper hand.
He who walks while holding hands
will live in loving tenderness.

March 4

When in initializing an upper tone
then you can demand
A strong, strong hand.

~ ~ ~

March 5

Be true to yourself
and hold onto your
Dreams.
For in all honest reality
you'll be fortified within
all your artistic abilities.

March 6

In one's life you
must feel
Content
In between
and you will
live on

In
Tranquility

~ ~ ~

March 7

Happiness is
ever promising and making
Extraordinary measures,
a part of your life.

March 8

Superior allusions can become
never-ending.
So make this day one
of all lasting moments
To your abilities worth
waiting for.

March 9

Devotion, dreaming
Realistic, Everlasting
all these add
up to you
are a true
Living human being.

March 10

Atmospheric, Materialistic and
simplicity will always be a part
within your well groomed
elegant fingers.

~ ~ ~

March 11

An ideal power follows
ultimately in your Path.
With Positive Influences
as you walk neath a
full gleaming moon.

~ ~ ~

March 12

The smallest
And
Greatest Gift of all
Is loving yourself.

~ ~ ~

March 13

Purity of words
can be your very Best friend.

March 14

Can you sit and wait for the sweetest bouquet;
to be held and viewed by your captive eyes.
For within this is the sweetest scent
of your beautiful eyes.

~ ~ ~

March 15

The best gift of all time is having all the
love and respect of your children.
On this special day you were gifted
with the talent of knowing your
Self-worth.

~ ~ ~

March 16

Enlist in the creativity within your mind.
Then this will broaden your intellectual being.
As if you were given an artistic goal of illusion.

~ ~ ~

March 17

Subliminal suggestions can enhance
beauty that surrounds you.
You love growing things
And watching them
all the steps of the way.

~ ~ ~

March 18

Lasting impressions can be your best friend.
With this thought keep your heart
all a glow in every step you initially take.

~ ~ ~

March 19

Stay and stand with a positive outlook then
your life will be well worth
all the gifts of time.

~ ~ ~

March 20

Poetically speaking: In this month
The spirit may Guide you to
A powerful transition
of purification
and tranquility.
Knowing this,
your own
Vision is the
Art within
Your soul.

~ ~

In so many years of your eminent seed
there will always be a beauty of a child
to which they have a love of watching
things grow from a tiny seed to the ripe
age of maturity. In your beautiful heart-beat
you'll be enriched with all the makings of
love with all because of your maturity of
your intellectual mind.

~ ~ ~

March 21

As for Aquamarine: This alone is
Utilized as a Mystical Sign for
All to sing And
Believe.

~ ~

March 22

With every fallen rain
It may bring in the brightness
Of showers.
For every string we play
Let's make music flow; fluently as every

Breath you breathe, we will sing
Beauty of Love's flair.

~ ~ ~

March 23

Upon This night
I'm belting out with song
As I look out the frosted window

March 24

As in your viewing eyes full Strong,
I hear the songs of sweet angels
Singing in harmony which belongs
Also in the distance by sweet baby Jesus thus
Will keep you warm along with in all
Your young journeys.

March 25

True artistic of beauty in
Songs so gloriously wrapped
Up in sweet smelling blankets which thus

Belong to the proud Mary as she had sang in song.
Brought all a magical feeling of how she felt
when she set her eyes upon her beauty of child.

March 26

Of all God's Children
You're enraptured
In awe of a purity of
knowledge and innocence.

March 27

When we all sing; sing of love with beauty
So strong within our captive hearts all day long.
Can you feel the rise of the tempo within
our lyric of songs of high tempo?

March 28

His Eminence
Does fill our hearts of Beauty
For unto his brethren breath

You'll be trusted in
Great uses of morality.

March 29

Beauty as we all sing along would be like a a true
Beauty has risen and born of the highest Powers.

March 30

When deep in thought can you behold
what your eyes right in front of you see.
Let there be no ulterior motive deep in your soul.

~ ~ ~

March 31

Dear Lord I have shed many a tear
For unto your loving arms,
you'll covet me with your charms.
As I now open my eyes I'm
blessed to know you'll always there for me.

SAPPHIRE

April's Child

You're like a raw cut
of a diamond
Glittering and smiling
Through all kinds of
Weather.

~ ~ ~

The beauty of
The flower
Within you
Flows like
Pink and purple
Of daisies and sweet peas
Your meaning
Is and always
Will be a

Great big curiosity
Of sweet pleasantries.

~ ~ ~

In ancient times the Romans
Gave this name its Latin name Aprilis
This is the season of allusion
It being the season when
Trees and flowers all open their
Fragrance upon earth's floral beauty.

~ ~ ~

April is the month to which
The goddess Venus was
Thus named Aphrodite to which back then
April was the second month of their year.

~ ~ ~

Thus the Romans utilized their powers of
Celebrating the birth of a child
Symbolizing their love as a relevance as gifts.

~ ~ ~

This specific flower the daisy
Was sent a hidden message of
romantic love as it was evolved.

~ ~ ~

In 450 BC the calendar year in
April had only 29 days.

~ ~ ~

When Julius Caesar was undertaken
he produced that April to have 30 days.

April 1

On this land of what we call dear
The one and only love is the love of your child.
As they grow up into adulthood they shall long
live and forever hold within them a love for their
mothers, fathers and other siblings along the way.

April 2

An intensifying beauty of land is
In your hands are held of fine wine

April 3

My dear Lord I feel
Your love inside of mine
I paint many a picture of you
From the heavens above.

April 4

With all thoughts of purest notions
Of your heavenly arms
Please keep me sheltered
And keep me warm;
Of your warmth within
I feel your loving arms.

~ ~ ~

On this blessed day
The Lord gave
Us your
Beloved heart.
Therefore we all shall treasure
You through all the walks in life,
as we walk on this beauty
Of land to which we call earth.

In all the world there has never been any
other and special person as of having the
love a very special lady to which we all
can say, "We love you Alice, mom, grand-mother
and beauty of an Oma."
Forever is my love to you sweet
and beautiful of what
I shall always say to you which
you have given us all what real love should be feeling
as a fine and eternal flame embedded
into us in every step we take.

We will always love you and adore
you for what you exemplify.

~ ~ ~

April 5

May any given day be all sweltered in heat
With all edible and fine elegant treasures
be within our tempting and well-defined
hands and eyes to have and to hold.

April 6

To touch my tearful heart
To be you're eternally loving
Crestfallen gal is yours as
I am singing of all beauty of songs.

April 7

In this life many have walked
through the sands of time
Upon this land of your divine

I may not at times even talked
Or had ventured out way to far.

April 8

As with fort tongue of thee as I walk
Upon this land of yours I do know
For you my dear I shall and do bestow,
Great beauty to everyone who has walked
and showed me gratitude along the way.

April 9

Great riches of wisdom upon this day
Shall last for as long as time lingers on
and also through the sands of time.

April 10

Let it be known throughout
every stepping stone may we
all be inspired with all loving
gifts with a happy destitution in life.

April 11

Heavenly Angels

May the angels in life be with you?
I hear them all singing soprano
Each and every one of them are blessed.
~ ~ ~
Within their divine arms
They brought forth
The beauty of you.
Knowing that your like
a daughter that your beautiful mother
has always adored you with her
tender loving heart and devotional
dreams of matters to which life has
to offer you along your chosen path in life.

April 12

With their heavenly angelic voices
God and the angels are within your reach
You are a majestic image of a girl
Let everyone rejoice and adhere to my speech.

~ ~ ~

April 13

Let there be few idle thoughts
Within each and everyone of us

For we all are not circumspect
To all of other people in life have
An equality of having a fine
educational background.

April 14

May you have a great deal of
courage in life and keep a calm
upper-tone of breath, for when you
speak out loud, then
maybe you will be forsaken.

April 15

For I bring forth great
Wishes of fortitude
I will never live in solitude
I am your humble pragmatic
individual soul for you.

We both shall reap with an
inner beauty held in the palm of our hands.

April 16

Believe In Yourself

Often in life a person does strife
And unknown to others you really can do
In some cases a man needs a wife
Who can work as hard like him to?
So with this said, may you both keep
to an even keel of belief within you.

April 17

The hills straight ahead
May not be ruggedly dead
For often in life, life's purpose
Can be steadily strenuous.

April 18

If you have the courage
Do not falter, for in life
You can be a well nourished
Individual and keep a stronghold
of proximity of knowing you can
Hold fast to your dreams.

April 19

Your dreams may come true
Your strength will lead
To greater accomplishments
Just learn to believe
And great things will come to you.

April 20

An all elusive dream
Can never compare
With you standing there

Don't you know?
You're mighty rare!

~ ~ ~

April 21

If by pure chance, which you may see
Above the skies, art all for human's thee,
With all your pride, you may enter right
Let truth be clear within your hearts delight.

April 22

Reach out to human's treasure
May your heart be enveloped?
With a fragment of a song for equal pleasure.

~ ~ ~

April 23

I heard the angels sing with joy
Their voices were filled with a lightness of love,
The stars and moon were dancing near

I heard the angels sing with sheer joy,
Their beautiful songs were meant for you.

~ ~ ~

April 24

May you be graced with rich's
of compassion?
Then you'll be greatly rewarded by being
Brought more pleasing thoughts
Within your bright eyes.

~ ~ ~

April 25

Beauty in Your Heart

In the bible on April 25 there is a
Quote that said,
"God had said he made everything beautiful"
Well my dear
He put beauty in
Your heart.

~ ~ ~

Once your proud parents brought
You home, their eyes were
Truly amazed as they looked into
Your beautiful loving eyes.
Your sweet little eyes were amazingly
touched as if the angels had kissed you
from up above all within the heavenly skies.

April 26

Beauty Surrounds All

Around the earth for all human life to see
Beauty surrounds our nature with hospitality
Comforting pleasures leads us to life's happiness
Delving warmth within our human's
loving embrace of soul
Energizing hope, love, faith and
courage to face another day
Fills our hearts with happiness and
with pure thought of gladness
Glorifying us with the gift of a
healthy and well balanced life
Helping all our families to live a
lightness and tranquil stay
Inspiration can be longevity's heart
and toil for all joys in strife
Jewels can bring many happy tears of
loving souls for all with thee

Knowing and having a happy
disposition on ones face to see
Loving one another for whom and
what we really truly are
Making every moment count
each and every day by far
Never letting anyone antagonizing
your own self-worth
Of your integrity and vast knowledge
as you live on earth
Please let your self-reliance be forever
known as truthful told
Quickly may you answer with
your exquisite love so bold?
Reaching far beyond your expertise
of beauty within you
Surely you'll be sheltering you and
your family with your view
Trustworthy you are and forever
be so ingratiatingly true
Unity will be your time to love
yourself for whom you'll win
Victory will be yours if you let love
enter your heart within
Willing words of wisdom can be on
your daily routine of whim
X-rated examples may reap within
your beautiful love of heart
Your loving children will never break
your beautiful heart apart

Zealously they'll treasure you to eternities
loving blessed days till the full end.

~ ~ ~

April 27

Integrity doesn't cost a dime but
Chivalry goes a long way
Let it be known as you are
lead into the right path
and true final destination
of having a knowledgeable mind.

~ ~ ~

April 28

Tonight upon this night
all the gems and stars from up
above are shining on all people on earth
to which all people can be enveloped with loving
arms and hopeful earnest words
of endearing love's matter.

~ ~ ~

April 29

Harvest moon glows neath
Lover's passions sweet love shows
Romance is intense

As you lay beside
Your loving partner in life
Beneath the shining stars.

~ ~ ~

April 30

All people here on this vast earth
Marvel at your handiwork of what it's worth,
How such coming from a tiny seed?

A blossoming flower appears full speed.
How can all those quaint little petals
Produce such a fragrance of medals,

Now standing so tall on beauty of our earth.
May you be adorned within thy soul?
Embrace your thoughts and savor beyond control.

~ ~ ~

AGATE

May's Child

You're like a
Lily of the valley
Your beauty of
Color is an
Intense color
Of
Emerald stone
Your heart is
Always filled with
Great humility.

~ ~ ~

Your vibrant intense
Happiness shall
Reign with all
Life's treasures
Of purity.

~ ~ ~

The many shades of green within the precious stone
Will be forever cherished within your hearts own.

May you reach into your sweet heart,
Which could be as well as a sip of fine wine.

~ ~ ~

Treasure these sweet pleasure's in
The month of May
For in this month, you'll be gifted
With all the love of your children.

May 1

May you reach within your
Intelligent mind
and learn to create
A well refined divine purpose.

~ ~ ~

May 2

Don't let your fears
Prevent you from

Doing what's right.
Just follow the right choice
And let others hear your voice.

~ ~ ~

May 3

Make gratuity part of your life.
Then you may be gifted by one
Sweetened and inviting along
each and every passing on to
the very next day.

May 4

Take time to find a fluent fountain of love
For thou soon shall be fitted with grace from above
For if you look up above you may
see a white shiny flying dove.

~ ~ ~

May 5

Remembering all your passions to which will bring
Like your magical smile for others so all will know
How true in depth of whom you really are.

~ ~ ~

May 6

Sing praises to all of life's treasured signs to be won
Like all devotions to which we all find hope, faith
And a piece of life's precious moments to love.

~ ~ ~

May 7

The cosmic forces when you were born
Had brought forth a true gemstone
To which he'll be treasured
Through all man-kind,
He has a true inscribed spiritual mind
And was inherited by the highest
priest to which we all truly adorn.

~ ~ ~

Sincerity, happiness and a creative
mind shall reap with,
All you can be in depth and rewarded for knowing.
That for you're my precious son, like the all allusive
Emerald Stone which shines so like an eternal
glimpse of a fiery stone which will bestow
and bring you beauty of all our earnest gifts?
Be steadfast and strong for your
heirs may live in longevity.

May 8

So many have trials hidden within
their interior domain
Be faithful with your thoughts
and be present with rewards of love in vain.

~ ~ ~

May 9

May you never be confused with the path you walk?
Let the divine power enter into your mind
So you can follow,
Your path in life.
With having no hidden agenda

then you'll be invited to leave a
tolerable meaningful life like a loving fella.

~ ~ ~

May 10

In all your daily rituals
May you walk a steady path!
And lavish within the colorful
Spring flowers that are in full
Blooming of fragrant hues
For onto your eyes
You may be quite mesmerized.

May 11

Your persona that resembles a rose
Flying beside you
A pretty angel I near
As if it were dipped
Like a glistening star.

May 12

Your love will be
sung through the
heavenly skies,
You have captured
My big brown eyes
Sending you candy kisses
Throughout endless of time.

Just remember you grand-mother loves
you with words that can even measure
up to her loving heart, be enraptured with
all that you meet up with in life and know
that you have an inner glow that reaches far
beyond the sparking stars and cosmic forces
Into your beautiful heart and soul

~ ~ ~

May 13

Watching you standing there
Standing so tall and lean
Your stance resembles
A fine statuette of a man.

May 14

May you be forever embraced?
With a happy constitution
Of vast knowledge
And a well -defined mind.

~ ~ ~

May 15

May you look upon all of the brightest stars?
And bring forth a vastness of tolerance for all to see.

~ ~ ~

May 16

May the all- consuming delightful
colors of the rainbow
Wrap you with happy thoughts and
exquisite love with sweet bliss.
For unto this day back in history,
your beautiful mother
Brought you in to this life, with much
hope and pure tranquility.

~ ~ ~

Long may you live in happiness
and be coveted with fruitful adoration
within every thing you do in life.

May 17

Let there be no cereal offerings. For in reality,
there will be no unraveled obligations.
Shall you reap with the sweetest!
Magical things that life has to give.

~ ~ ~

May 18

Let not fear enter into your soul;
for in all capacity you'll be
greatly rewarded with human humility.

~ ~ ~

May 19

As the night darkens, comes a new dawning
Of the harvest moons domineering path.
Among many voyageurs, they traverse afar and view

The magnitude of wealth in earth's finest rewards.
Keeping and being true to yourself
Let there be no lies within
Your beautiful heart.

~ ~ ~

May 20

Many people seem to be so adept or then adopt
when changing their idle memories with
thoughts, through human tribulations.

~ ~ ~

May 21

May you never quarrel with a rich man?
For he may make you pay a
penance for your downfall.
Or shall I say he may make you
rich beyond all means.

~ ~ ~

May 22

Be so very kind to all who may surround you
Then they'll be justified by your
knowledgeable skills.

~ ~ ~

May 23

May there be sovereignty throughout our land
For those who hold a majestic
attitude could become a ruler.

~ ~ ~

May 24

If you follow an influential man, be sure to be
Wise of his many well- mannered attributes.

~ ~ ~

May 25

May you never insult a person's intellect?
For a wise mind and tongue
knows when not to talk.

~ ~ ~

Upon this magnificent earth there
stands a well mannered-man
So tall and lean, which came from
abroad to this beauty land of ours
With the magical things and
tribulations he had accompanied
A surreal home and lavished on to
his children a maturity of
knowledge beyond his knowledgeable mind.
He brought forth four beautiful
children which will be
forever greatful of having a fine
upstanding father, his high
intellect was always known through
his fine statuette of being
A firm believer in doing all things
right in every thing
they start and do to the finer things in life.

May 26

Am I seeing and viewing stardust in your eyes?
Your beauty within keeps me hypnotized.

~ ~ ~

May 27

In this land before all time
There hath been a queen that had
Brought forth an equal opportunist,
To which all your mother's had
To be so spiritual to keep
You within your God- fearing loving arms.

~ ~ ~

Let an open door enter your soul
Then show forth and you will have to
Keep honesty and perseverance within all your
Thoughts and this shall be you're greatest
Gift of all.

May 28

May you reign in the powers within your view!
Then you'll be able to extend your virtues so true!

~ ~ ~

May 29

Waste, not a minute for
Thy gift of life can
Hold a divine power
Which enhances your
Well- defined heart.

~ ~ ~

May 30

The marching of your steps
Can be heard with
A pure and honest love
And caring heart.

~ ~ ~

May 31

Beneath the starry nights below
You were blessed with a gifted pen.
Let all the words flow as your
Chosen words may ring so true.

~ ~ ~

Forever and unto this land which brought
forth us this creation of May flowers
To enhance this greenery of grounds
of delight and fragrant of sight.

~ ~ ~

May is when all our beloved mother's
do have a special day
For all us children or adult children
can and send them all our love
To always love them and cherish them,
throughout their long days
With laughter and enjoyment within our precious
thoughts to have and to hold.

~ ~ ~

And unto many chosen paths
May all the people on earths fallen lands
Bring forth a joyous heart
Of sweet harmonious songs.

~ ~ ~

Upon entering in the middle
month of the year, brings
Forth the milestone which for all shall prevail.
For unto the next chapter all may be blessed
Within all their impurities within
their intellectual mind.

~ ~ ~

AGATE

June's Child

You're like a gem
Of a pearl
Siting in wait
Like the endless
Rose which
May be
Encased
By the sting
Of thorns.

~ ~ ~

Of the other
Flower
Is the Honeysuckle
Your other
Stone of birth contrasts
Like the moonstone.

Brings forth
A beautiful meaning
Of how friendships
Can last.

~ ~ ~

June 1

June reaps all leafy tunes
Which brings for the a quiet of
All musical songs.
You see the angel rays
They're hovering near
To protect you dear!

~ ~ ~

June 2

Blissful, tearful sweet lasting memories
Can bring forth great comfort inside
And know you'll have a vastness
Of treasure in thoughts
For an unlimited time.

~ ~ ~

June 3

This month is in the middle of the year
to which you may have many ventures
to cross, let no man be the better of you
forever in your heart is like a piercing sword.
Take the time to reflect and make each day
an inviting gift of gaiety, as it can be
your ever-lasting goal in life.

~ ~ ~

Then as your days are long gone
Unto your chosen path let
The Lord make amends
Your heart in all the lands
And walk in your final destination
of your chosen life.

June 4

For all the unknown forces within this month
Can interfere to heal your empathy towards
Your fellow men and brothers.

~ ~ ~

June 5

As all things have been told in ancient
biblical time in the center of the
Year caused a ripple effect
to all the unknown forces
From the great beyond of
all the celestial stars.

June 6

Let there be no barriers left to cross
For with not having a pure heart can
bring forth an ill-fated disease.
Open up to all matters of your heart
Then all will be rewarded by what
you will eventually reap.

~ ~ ~

June 7

In ancient Roman history your moonstone was
Believed that the goddess Diana was enclosed within
the stone. This stone was believed to change in
appearance, until the 16th century.

~ ~ ~

June 8

In ancient mythology they believed that dewdrops
Fell from the heavens and fell
into the depth of the sea.

~ ~ ~

June 9

In ancient scripture of India; many great
warriors encrusted their swords
With pearls to symbolize the meaning of
tears and sorrows of warrior swords.

~ ~ ~

June10

The depth of a swordsman can have
A charismatic move
As like the fastest Ninja man.
Make no mistake for seeing
And viewing this man can
Be in the very depth of you.

~ ~ ~

June 11

Kept within a shellfish of one's mind,
Can cause a ray of sunshine to enter in.
There for let all the beauty of rays
Enter into the sight of you.

~ ~ ~

June 12

With your aptitude of cheerfulness, your beliefs
Will grant you all of well wishes of
New beginnings and respect of pure heart.

~ ~ ~

June 13

Through ancient biblical times,
Brought forth a firm foundation
Of ancient rituals powers to which
Would cleanse and heal their wounds.

June 14

Let no man ever belittle you for
You have a force within you
To be able to stand your ground
And knowing your limit
Will be your true loving giving gift:
as held within the palm of your hand.

~ ~ ~

June 15

This month is full of hope, love and many
Constructive forms of happiness.
For knowing whom you really are
Can harvest your love by going the extra mile.

June 16

The greatest gift to all man- kind
Is in the farthest reaches of your mind.

~ ~ ~

June 17

All simple pleasures in life are so realistically free
So keep all the simple things in life
within your arms reach.

~ ~ ~

June 18

Read one sentence in a book each day; then
Knowing and use this as a learning
tool to educate your mind.

~ ~ ~

June 19

Tell many truths instead of lies,
then you'll be pardoned
By God's blessings of entering
into the heavens above.

~ ~ ~

June 20

By living in a controversial atmosphere,
your proverbial attitude
will be well nourished in longevity's realm.

June 21

Keep positivity as the mainstream in your life.
Then all will be given a well treasured path.

~ ~ ~

June 22

Don't be hypercritical to others you cross,
for they may be involved with an extreme measure.
Don't be so anal and try to exempt your mind
can be your own worst enemy.
Just keep in mind the best thing you can
offer is having a firm and happy constitution
in all your endeavors within your frame of mind.

June 23

Investing the powers within your mind
Will bring forth great knowledge and intelligence.

~ ~ ~

June 24

Scarlett petals flow very sweetly towards your view.
Now their laying right next to you.

~ ~ ~

June 25

When doing the Polonaise dance you
must wear a short-sleeved over-dress
Then your stately being shall be
rewarded many times so few.
Note (this type of dress attire goes
back to ancient Roman times)

~ ~ ~

In many so long and painless walks of life,
Let there be known that in your life's measure is
Like a falling of stone, and never wreck sweet havoc
Onto all that you know and cross.

~ ~ ~

Upon this daily routine you're many
Children may live on in sweet longevity,
They'll always treasure the path you've walked on.

June 26

May you walk with-in the beauty of your soul?
As if you could touch mine
With a graceful kind
A feathery touch.

~ ~ ~

June 27

An ounce of prevention
Can aspire to give you great courage.

~ ~ ~

June 28

Do not let failure
enter your mind

Make SUCCESS
Your biggest
MOTIVATOR !!

June 29

Creating an ocean of
Great possibilities;
Using and cherishing
Your imagination so
Be creatively wise.

~ ~ ~

Also on this day many who have sought to
Brighten their anniversaries of love's
Compassionate door.
Let not one soul befall
your beloved one's mind.

June 30

Belief in one's self and
Earning a fruitful living
Life can be a beautiful and
Carefree thought.

~ ~ ~

ONYX

July's Child

Fair sparks as
The smashing ruby
As seen with in
Form like the
Water lily, or
Shades of Larkspur
Bring the meaning
Of your royal
Purple and also pink.
Lies in the
True meaning of
your gaiety
and opens your heart
with strong levity.

~ ~ ~

Be fruitful to all
And you'll reap
With sweet
Rhapsodies

~ ~ ~

May the comfort
Of your soul
Be filled with
The joys of
Love, grace
And true meaning
For you were born
With the grace
Of being an intelligent
Human being.

~ ~ ~

This July's child loves in
honor and
Pure devotion
She's happy with all the simplicity
to all
What matters within her beautiful heart!

~ ~ ~

While I propose to a well measure of words
May you harken to all love's treasured
Sweet blessings.

~ ~ ~

As your walk in life has been set in stone
You'll be fortified with the greatness
of true knowledge.

~ ~ ~

July 1

In every one's path
Enrichment of one's purpose in,
venting and letting all your worries to depart.
Evolving in life can create love in your heart.
Just let everyone know the truth then it can
be known to all and you'll be
forever set free.

~ ~ ~

July 2

May your guidance be within your
precious voice to be forever told?
In your many walks in life
All will treasure your gifted talents.
So please inherit of keeping
your love invested
With all your companions

within their strengths in mind
forever told.

~ ~ ~

July 3

Keep an affordable solution
Within arms reach
Then you'll be thinking
Of the color peach.

~ ~ ~

July 4

Let perseverance be your guiding light
In all matters within your heart.

July 5

As foretold by a choice of an old friend
Discarding a new one cannot equal the one you lost.

~ ~ ~

July 6

A poor man's wisdom may not inflict intelligence
Knowing and hearing may he not be criticized.
For he may be wiser than you.

July 7

Do not let misery enter your soul for
This may lead to a captive sorrow.
And not to be able to move
on in many more special
Thoughts of all your family.

~ ~ ~

July 8

A pure man knows no ultimate pain
For within his pure heart he shall reign.

~ ~ ~

July 9

Some afflictions brings forgetfulness
Of past most precious delights.

~ ~ ~

July 10

A pure man may not appear as like
A caged in bird, yet he may be
Inflicted by a woman scorned.
For he may never meet a woman
with pure nobility within
her loving heart.

~ ~ ~

July 11

As strength gives off
A meaningful relativity
Be constructive
To all of nature's lands
of transparency.

~ ~ ~

July 12

Let a human devotion contain
You're warm inviting heart
As you take solace with
Your partners love
For she or he
Will treasure your
Romantic heart for
All you're really worth.

~ ~ ~

July 13

The true meaning of
Life lies with
Honesty within your heart.

~ ~ ~

Thus brought on to this earth
A beautiful baby girl with eyes so
Precious and captive when you
Look into her face. Her soft angelic
face had blossomed into a Petal
Of Scarlett which will one
Day be so blessed with a
noble and pure heart.

~ ~ ~

July 14

Your self-preservation has been your greatest
Gift to all of your beloved kin.

~ ~ ~

July 15

Any man or woman who pierces
their partner's heart
Can be as contemptible as a swordsman's sharp,
Piercing end, let not what they shall be
Inflicted with so much hatred.
So make the first move
And remove that hatred in your broken heart.

~ ~ ~

July 16

True beliefs can enter into your heart
Make each day a magical moment in time.

~ ~ ~

July 17

Loving and enter into a new day dawning
Sing sweet appraisals to all the winged birds.
As they may be flying up into the great skies above.

~ ~ ~

July 18

Sitting and reflecting of human nature's
Sweet wine can enter a calming effect to unwind.

July 19

The multi of colors underneath the full moon
Is like the all- consuming
electrifying glowing embers.

~ ~ ~

July 20

Let no man harden your strength of determination
For he who does is of a liability of weak in haste.

July 21

Sometimes little birds fly in circles of late
Which I've heard the sky-larks sing.
Within this happy tune
Is the very beginning
Of a personal goal
Be strong and you will win.

~ ~ ~

July 22

With joyous thoughts upon this day
A sunshiny attitude will always display
The true beauty upon your face.

July 23

You may encounter the biggest dragonfly
Which does bring forth a new rebirth of a child,
Upon starting a new beginning in life.
This remarkable human being is the gift
of being invited upon your loving eyes.

July 24

May your inner-tolerance forever be kept
In tune with the many mood-swings in your heart.
Try to keep them in tune with sweet realities bliss.

July 25

On this day that you were born
The angels brought forth
An angelic kiss with
The lightest feather
Of love on your
Well defined hands
And grace on your
pure little face.

~ ~ ~

The goddess of love
Is dearly in your
Pure heart,
For you are
Definitely
A woman wise.
The gracious beauty
Your mother gave you
Was her all well treasured
Gifted heart of love.

~ ~ ~

There lies within
Your beautiful eyes
The greatest gift of all
A true beautiful woman
In everything you say and do
A well-defined woman
With all God's hands
Touching you with
His blessed tranquil
depth of LOVE.

July 26

In this month of July the favor of
The moon will be enhancing your beauty
Upon a well treasured stone.
This stone is like starting
A new beginning well worth
What you've been waiting for.

July 27

Your true gift lies within your sweetness
Of breath with each and every given day
Of the many days, months and years ahead.

July 28

On this blessed day your mother gave you
The greatest gift of all,
The beauty of you.

July 29

Mind your manners and you shall reap with
A mild mannered-man within your treasured heart.

~ ~ ~

In your many walks in life, you have been
Blessed within God's loving arms
With the strongest of fortitude to which you
Have walked in each step and breath you've taken.

July 30

Upon this night the stars from up above
Will be shining on you tonight as
You'll always be enveloped with all life has and
will bring beauty unto you.

July 31

There lies within a full moon, the many happy songs
Of all nature's calls of the wild animals singing
To the all allusive of the bluest of the moons
Delightful surprise the dawning of the new moon.

~ ~ ~

Forever is the child that is born in this month
Of July will always be wrapped in a soft pillow
Of the softest clouds that have flown by along
With the white dove of endearing love.

~ ~ ~

Be always known as the first beginning
An all inviting of the coming of Autumn breezes:
Thus beginning the merry month of August kisses:
This novel of an idea will be forever told
Unto all your late and future ancestors
The sweetest stories ever told.

PERIDOT

August's Child

Is like a gem of a peridot
(lime-green) which is
What Cleopatra
Wore upon her warm
Gifted love's chest.

~ ~ ~

This stone has great
Healing powers and
Brings forth
The strength of love's
Treasured longevity.

~ ~ ~

The stone of this month
Has been with
The best of Egyptians

99

of
Royalty.

~ ~ ~

This beauty of stone was used as a talisman in the
Days of pirates to ward off many all evil entities

~ ~ ~

Of all things beautiful, the
Blessings born upon this
Child was when your loving
Mother brought you her
Loving hands and joy
With just one moment
When she looked into
Your soft angelic
Smile on this
Special day on earth
Till the end
Of time.

~ ~ ~

In the palm of your
Hand from this day forward
Till the lord walks on
the softened sands of earth,

Long live the many impurities to be lifted
From the great songs above,
Your daily thoughts through life's
Divine purpose will bring

Forth all the beauty on earth
As seen through only your eyes.

Aug. 1

Of the sun, this stone
Has great powers
Of prosperity, dignity
And is known as the
"Evening Emerald

~ ~ ~

Aug. 2

My heart will beat to the greatest gift of all
the beat of love's romantic song

~ ~ ~

Aug. 3

Believing in one's self -reliance
makes life's purpose healthy calm
and greatly rewarded.

~ ~ ~

Aug. 4

Be satisfied with what life's offer and
take a chance to believe in true love

Aug. 5

Don't under -estimate the powers
of your parents love for you.
For you'll always be their precious child in any given
Age to which they truly adore and love you.

Aug. 6

Uncovering the many shadows in your mind,
will entice the greatest learning abilities
Let the many knowledge and wise
Enter into your divine mind.

~ ~ ~

Aug. 7

Don't under estimate the power of reading
Let there be a great knowledge of
Capacity in your fruitful
And broadening mind.

~ ~ ~

Aug. 8

Truth be told in honesty's breath
A fond moment of a fresh man's responsibility
Can never cause any ripples into
A beautiful mind.

~ ~ ~

Aug. 9

Then along comes an angel of a song
Which makes the heavens well-
muted with sweet bliss.
All that is saying your gallantry
will be forever kissed.

~ ~ ~

Aug. 10

When the angels brought forth your beautiful eyes
He gave them an equal measure of sweet enterprise.

~ ~ ~

Aug. 11

At the descending moon above
Their lies the crimson of the moon's love
Their first born child which upon
Was born of beauty so bright!
Of so many years ago
Which in another four month's
Our blessed Jesus came.

~ ~ ~

Aug. 12

In the many months ahead
there lies in wait a firm foundation
of a man who may be considered
to be our next Emperor of longevity's
interior ruling light on earth.

Aug. 13

Sing joys throughout each day with
Your beautiful partner in life.

~ ~ ~

Aug. 14

Sing and all will sing with you in
Magical tune within your sweetened
Beautiful and passionate of heart.

~ ~ ~

There has been a new creation of a new baby girl
So bright that of an angelic beauty upon
Its beautiful loving mother's arms
Her name is Kenzi Alice Hemmerling-Baird

Aug. 15

You have been embedded with a true kind heart
And a glorious happy fruitful days ahead.

Aug. 16

Treasure all these days ahead, and make
Every minute count with a positive frame of mind.
Then with this statement remember to live
With an up-beat state of mind.

Aug. 17

In life's journey may your pockets fill:
With many happy memories and knowing
That you're so very well loved.

Aug. 18

On this day in history, your mother and father
Became the proud parents of you!!

Aug. 19

Think not that all is lost
But think that all is at minimum cost.

And by in looking through the looking glass
Then many times over you'll be lived and loved with
by your beautiful one of she or he
has a great amount of class.

Aug. 20

The closer you get as you approach unto me
The closer I feel as I look into your eyes so true.

Aug. 21

Let there be no unknown barriers in between
As we're both walking along so happy and care-free!
Then we'll both walk on through all to see
Of how life can bring a well blessing in disguise.

Aug. 22

In Hawaii, this precious stone
of the peridot was also
Known as a symbol of the tears to which the

Goddess Pele, had worn and had
a yellowish tinge to it.
She kept on to hang it so very close to her heart.

Aug. 23

Upon entering the changes of
the celestial stars above
One can see the epitome of how the cosmic forces
Have been forever seen through all eyes
Of all the grace of the wild-habitats on earth.

Aug. 24

In earliest Egyptian Times the queen Cleopatra
Had been the highest grace to please her
True destiny.

Aug. 25

This month is filled with great wonders of
How predominant how our earth had
Been known through all the sands of time.

Aug. 26

On the day that you were born
Came an angel that said onto me;
He'll be so very gracious within
His tiny heart and achieve
Great wisdom within his true heart.

~ ~ ~

The very essence of your view
Has been with the mighty forces
Of how nature and son became
Encrusted with this precious gemstone
As a cosmic attribute within
God's Nature of Land.
For knowing you and as I held
you so close to my tender loving
arms when I first set eyes on you
was worth all the complexities
of having you in my life.

Aug. 27

Knowing when to stop and smell all
Floral scents, can reach within
Your visual artistic side.

Aug. 28

Autumn colors does bring sweet wonder
Upon one's viewing eyes.

Aug. 29

Knowing and viewing all
the great aspects of your life
Will bring sweet music to all that are
blessed in with greatness of strife.

Aug. 30

The closer you get as you approach unto me
The closer I feel as look into your eyes so true
Let there be no unknown barriers in between
As we're both walking along so happy and free!

Aug. 31

As I sit here tonight playing this flute
I've heard all the sweet angels all sing

In the heavens so very cute.
They're also playing their
Harps for all ears to hear.
Their all -consuming melodic tune upon the
Nature's path and skies so clear in view.

The ending of this month comes
to be a new dawning
Of all that will ginger on all the fine and domestic
Fragrant colors of this beauty of autumnal
weather thus is beauty that forever is bound.

All the ancient God's through all
mythology have brought forth
Great knowledge to enter into any
realm of our habitual earth.
Which has made us the society we are today.
Whether there be wars, lightened
souls of happiness or to reach,
beyond our pure hectic lives.
Therefore, we all can learn to be
a teacher to one and all.

~ ~ ~

There is a royal beauty bright
In all the world you're in the extreme light
If everyone could see what I see on this night
The true beauty of love's pure delight.

CARNELIAN

September's Child

Resembles a
Sapphire like
The morning glory
A multitude of
Pure devotion,
Resonates of
The color pink and
Is laced with
purple hues

~ ~ ~

The daintiness of your light
Is filled with hope, love
and desire all
Is like a joy of
Happiness.

~ ~ ~

Your mother gave you
Her gifted talent
like the talented
Artist Van Gogh;
Make all
Your artistic
Endeavors and
establish your eagerness.

Sept. 1

The artifacts of life
Are like the powers within your heart
Make all that you know become like
The wild-flowers among nature's toes.

~ ~ ~

Sept. 2

It never ceases to amaze me of
how your many sails in life
Can catch so many pleasant
pleasing fish as you wish.

For cannot you hear the singing lark sing
Please lord of all the seas bring forth
Much vastness a fresh load of full-fresh fish.

~ ~ ~

Sept. 3

As my eyes are seeing all glazing eyes
While they are all watching the tangerine sunset
For many have seen your delightful eyes,
memorize what's in front of you.

Sept. 4

I'm seeing all the glitter that you still wear
As you walk by in with your style
like a quaint of flair.

Sept. 5

Like a softened kiss of a feather
As it cascades like a breath of fresh air
It's now clearly sailing upon the evolving sphere.

Sept. 6

May you for-ever be compressed into a page
Into a lavender of an illustrated book
For all of eternity to read as in for all time
Which you eternally will look
As left like an eternal gift given to you
To have and to hold forever within your view.

Sept. 7

They say that time may heal all hurtful wounds
Like in this beautiful precious month
of September in full bloom.
The magical feeling and seeing
all the beauty of leaves
Turning into the mulch of colorful
leaves like tangerine
And so many other colors too.

Sept. 8

They say that man cannot be a like a mirror
The very essence of mind and common peers.
Shall be the very embodiment of how their,
Life can turn into something else. Like

the blink of an eye, your so far beyond
Inviting us to be seen with grace of debonair.

Sept. 9

I'm like a willful doll sitting and
waiting for you to come home
Just how long do you think that I can
hold onto my delightful eyes!
Knowing how you always seem to
work long endless nights
Seeing you walk through the
front door does bring on
a wonder of delightful colors of sweet matter.

Sept. 10

The only thing that they may be able to control
Is their many choices within their hearts and soul?

Sept. 11

May it either be right nor wrong?
The lasting moments will always linger on.

Of all how life can be stronger in depth
Of our intellectual mind.

Sept. 12

Can you not find neither foe nor friend?
For I wish that you'll never have to pretend.
Knowing how to be vocal can be the best
thing a human can bring forth.
A well- established mind and voice.

Sept. 13

Sometimes the long and endless nights and days
will forever stay within your so inviting face?
I see all the love be so in graced
Of all that you are truly blessed.
An etiquette of fine finesse.

Sept. 14

September sweet dancing onto our velvety lawn
As we dance and romance all night till dawn,
While we both sing of magical songs.

Sept. 15

I'd gladly throw away all my treasured gifts
Just to see your sweet smiling inviting lips.
There will be no long ending good-byes
For we were always be meant for each other.

Sept. 16

Home is where you lay your fallen hat
Can make coming home a sweetened love call,
Of all what life has to offer, is our sweet
And loving home of homes.

Sept. 17

Rhapsodies kiss as we sit on under the full moon
Will make us feel like we're both in earnest tune.

Sept. 18

By my sweet happy petal of rose
and let us bring sweetened

Loveliness into our passionate of
rose-petals on our bed
As we're both in sync with our
voluptuous desire of wedded bliss.

Sept. 19

May you embrace the leaves?
Which flourishes in autumn
A floral scented of chords.

Sept. 20

Tis the season for wanting to marry
Just be happy with your gracious of merry.
For sometimes in life's treasured journeys
you may be enveloped with all of loves happiness.

Sept. 21

All mother's across the bounteous of lands
Are all off to sending their young
one's back to school.
Sometimes they may be glad to sending them off

or they may be frightened in being left home alone.

Sept. 22

At this time of fall all creatures big or small
Are all searching for new homes to sleep
Into the beginning of the early spring dew.

Sept. 23

Memories of so long ago
Does make all minds think of
The first fall of snow.
Hoping and wishing that it
Will come later so we won't have to
Start shoveling snow so soon.

Sept. 24

Time to get all things wrapped into one
Tis for next month is coming to lighten
Up for the great Halloween Pumpkin
Will be scaring all young little ones

To all run on home with much delights
of sugar sweetened lollipops.

Sept. 25

Imagination is like an all consuming
Cherished thoughts of creating magical
Oceans of possibilities.

Sept. 26

On this day that you were born
Your special dear mother
Had not even sworn
To love, coddle and treasure this
Moment for all the days of Eternal
Mothers of smothering of kisses.

Sept. 27

Make a certainty to follow the direction
Of confidence within your dreams.

Sept. 28

In each and every individual in life, we all
Have a different story to tell and read
To all our beloved fathers and moms.

Sept. 29

As we both walk along on the sands of time
We're both holding our hands with love in rhyme.
Can you not find my intense desire to keep walking?
On these long and endless hot times on hot sand.

Sept. 30

Dearest man that holds my passions
within his hard woven hands
We'll keep on walking to many long
endless roads in vast lands.
He's sitting and waiting for his precious first born
To come into this world without a worry of worn.
Here comes a new dawning of
the up-coming months
For all people on earth will be in bounteous cheer.

This month ahead is filled with happy magical sights

Of all sugars, candies, and popcorn too
Here's bringing good Cheer to
the Month of October

~ ~ ~

This is the season for much multiple vibrant colors
For this lively month was established
since the early days of
when, the Virgin Mary had all
the suns surrounding
Her graciousness neath the sacred sun and stars
For her "Winning Grace."
Had been graced
Upon our
Heavenly father
Jesus.

~ ~ ~

Upon those times the beauty of the Calendula
which also considered,To be called the Marigold.
In ancient times, these precious floral flowers
Were strung out in garlands and kept by all
Humans front door; this illustrated to be
Protecting the inhabitants to which they
Once lived to ward off evil spirits.

~ ~ ~

Another belief was to put these majestic flowers
Under the bed which would give the sleeping
Individual to have visionary dreams.

~ ~ ~

The multitude of this month is so educational
For all to equate to in this life. Even the color
Of their birthstone is one of a reliable
Stone which could often change its color.
When the wearer wore this it was believed
To indicate the mental state and health
Of one who was wearing it.

~ ~ ~

To which had become the many exotic
Minds to be held in the powerful soft
Belief of hope, faith, and innocence
Of the child or adult.
In ancient roman time the people
Had Christened the Opal,
"Anchor of Hope."

~ ~ ~

There brought forth a divine
Intervention of the coming of
An invisible and powerful talisman
To keep all evil entities away
From entering into their quiet domain.
This statement has been worded and written
About through all the depth of time since the
Beginning to which before our Jesus was born.

~ ~ ~

BERYL / OPAL

October's Child

Has brought forth a precious of
Divinity of love beyond the
Empowering stars.
This star
Lies
Into the highest
Constellation which not one
Human can see within
their eyes only
One may have
To use
A
Telescope
To see the luminous glow.

~ ~ ~

This purity of stone was known
To have fallen into the
Depth of the sea.
One would have to swim into
The depth of the deep blue sea
Or the use of the fishing
Net as oft they had to use.

~ ~ ~

The very essence of this beauty of stone was worn
Onto many rulers which was
encrusted in their Crowns;
thus protecting them from
Evils and unknown Enemies. As the story goes
the word opal, was derived from
Roman term, Opalus. The word
was at one time referred to as:
Oops, which then signified
She was the Goddess of fertility.

~ ~ ~

Oct. 1

As the story goes and written of so long ago
In this beautiful month, comes to all through out
many lands. The relativity of this divine intervention
of this month has been told so many legends of old.

In this delightful month there
lies many people which
has a softness stream of purity and love. The
very essence of life and beauty upon others.

Oct. 2

Then came upon an experiment of true nobility
Of the goddess Cleopatra who had worn a
set of magnificent Opals to attract
Mark Anthony to her, the ruler of Rome.

Oct. 3

And onto this night a beauty of a baby was born
The baby kept her mom's eyes in sweet
Adoration for once her eyes opened
They seemed to look right at her.
Her mother knew from first
Sight; she'd always be treasured.
I heard her calling her name.

~ ~ ~

In all matters of the heart, her eyes
Had been transformed with a
Softened glow like a baby of

An open opal.
Her transparency was like a little gift
Sent from above like the whitest of
A dove with a heart shaped pearl.

Oct. 4

There is a magical feeling in the air
To which all is under a feeling of no despair
To reach into the farthest reaches of our vast
Galaxies upon our celestial stars.

Oct. 5

Walk with a hopeful heart in stride
For in knowing this you'll be walking
With much clarity in your mind.

Oct. 6

When upon entering an unknown path
Keep in mind all that thus surrounds you.
For you may get lost.

Oct. 7

When you were brought into this world
Your mother and father were already
In love with your little compact heart.

Oct. 8

Into the farthest reaches of your mind
Let not one person belittle your talented arts.

Oct. 9

In the mainstream of life all the simple
pleasures are free.

Oct. 10

Always remember to tell someone you care
In moments like this they'll understand.

Oct. 11

Make a firm foundation within your heart
Of becoming a wise and noble
person of individuality.
Let everyone be welcoming a comment
to one you really care about.

Oct. 12

My beloved heart
Will wait and smile with
A magical view in your eyes.
Your mother and father brought
Home a beauty of son, was treasure of
Like the brightest sun.

You will always be loved within both by
In their beautiful hearts, you're one
Very special boy to know always
That they have been blessed
Within a compassion beyond your young
And delightful eyes, you're the happiest
Song upon their loving eyes.

~ ~ ~

Oct. 13

In heavens warm arms
Let they be wrapped
Around your beloved
Body with enchanting music.

Oct. 14

As seen above into the clouds tonight
The all enticing wonders of precious sight.
The floral scents of the autumn breeze
Does make all the beauty of sweet memories.
The beauty of your ever sweet soul has brought
Forth two beautiful children with
hearts filled with gold.

Oct. 15

Here lies a gracious beauty bright
A beloved one of purest sight
A true reminder that we
All shall sing of magical
Songs of love
That last and

Last forever
More.

Oct. 16

On this night that you were born
Mom and Dad brought forth a
Beauty bright; all wrapped up in
Tender blankets of wonders of love,
You remind me of that flying dove.

~ ~ ~

Into the light that you left us all so
early in your beautiful life with a longing
for each of us to be lead into your peaceful
eyes and keep us all safe as we all wept for you.
May we all be within your warm heavenly arms
My beloved sister Lynda you'll be forever with
our lord and creator of love till
we meet with you again.

~ ~ ~

Oct. 17

I can see and feel the honesty in your heart
Your proud parents loved the person you've become.

A star above had lit so bright it
sparkled like a diamond bright.

Oct. 18

When walking and dancing can you feel?
Like Fred Astaire had waltzed on clouds so rare.
The sheer delight of this scene in our eyes
Makes our hearts feel like a feather light.

Oct. 19

On seeing a sight of pure delight
A shooting star which I found so bright.
This brought a beautiful image for all to see
And make a wish for many to keep in hearts of glee.

Oct. 20

The many trees are swaying in the breeze
Like a magician is making their dancing leaves.
To entice the many singing birds to nest within
The beauty of the autumn breeze.

Oct. 21

On this day in history their
Is a saying that goes you were blessed!
Within a treasured heart that
Resembles a well -shaped
Gift of art.

Oct. 22

On the day that you were born
All the angels came and sang
With their angelic tunes
Your big beautiful eyes
Sure did glow with
All the love in your
Mother's eyes.

Oct. 23

Tis coming near the end of October
When all little children are waiting
Patiently to go trick or treating
Oh, how they all will be dressed
Up and looking, walking with

Much energy, can their
Parents even keep up.

Oct. 24

There is a feeling in the air that many
People like to get married in this month
The multicolored leaves brings out the
Best in life like a treasure chest filled with love.

Oct. 25

There will be many trails to walk upon
As when a hunter thus had driven on.
The star-spangled birds are long past gone
Now all that's left are bigger animals to hunt.

Oct. 26

There will be many more mountains to climb
Onto endlessly while you harness
all your necessities.
Make your goal to leap and reap then
you'll be able to climb much higher.

Oct. 27

You've been a blessing in disguise to everyone
Who truly knows your intense beautiful heart!

Oct. 28

All little girls and boys are all getting excited for
Halloween is getting so very close;
Better watch out for not getting
too many toothaches.

Oct. 29

Analogy of a writer and a poet
They both have a great imagination.
Without a great imagination
May they never fall long and hard.

Oct. 30

Better start worrying and start to chain up
All your dogs and treasures. Nearing the

Night all little children are getting too
Excited to go to sleep for they,
All want to go trick or treating.

Oct. 31

As all little children are sent to school
They all have one thought in mind.
They're all getting excited to dress
Up like princess's, goblins or any
Other character even little
Mickey Mouse would do.
Or even like Indiana Jones
That's all what they will do.

~ ~ ~

Onto the next day, they will be or
May not be well rested, for into
Their tiny tummies, may be hurting
From all those sweets, candies and
Even potato chips.

~ ~ ~

Onto the month of November
There are so many more stories to tell.
Of winter wonder-land can be so much fun
Like making snowmen and sliding down hills
With smiles on their eyes and singing with cheer.
Tis the time of the season with laughter in hearts.

~ ~ ~

On this beautiful November's month
Two stones which had been worn
By the royal emperors which was
A symbol of the Egyptian Sun God Ra.
This stone was the color topaz which
Held a fiery intensity: brilliant fibers
Thus brought brilliant golden glow.

~ ~ ~

Has been a precious stone to which all
Had been given blessed healing power;
As for on the more gentle qualities has
Given this sweet little child a gentle,
Peaceful air of loyalty prosperity and
The greatest gift of all creativity.
In this blessed child there lies
A prowess on the wearer a
Clear thought of reality.

~ ~ ~

TOPAZ

November's Child

You were blessed and bestowed
The great knowledge of clarity.
Your passionate desires
Holds a spiritual belief to which
Your heart is one made
Of a great genteel nobility.

~ ~ ~

You drink in from the depth of your mind
A veracious attitude and are quite
Protective of your beloved one's.
In your qualities of wisdom since
The dawn of your twin birth
Stones shows you're a materialistic
Kind of man or woman that leaves
Nothing untouched and always
Knows how to finish all with
Your fine exquisite hands.

~ ~ ~

In past of so many long years ago
Your precious gemstone was once known as
The Quartz of Healing Stone.
He who wears this stone shall be cured
If they have health problems dealing
With the unlikeliness of kidney's disease.

Of all legends in biblical times
The citrine promoted vitality and energy
To whom ever wears it.
According to Chinese feng, in the philosophy,
Citrine creates an abundance of health and wealth.
Your other color which is Topaz, illustrates
Its potency which will bestow
intelligence and strength
And also has a deep sign of love and affection.
In your mother's eyes you'll always be thought
Of her little precious son and knowing this
Her heart is full of love and devotion
For she treasures you as her little Russian Czar.
Note: this is just a noted expression.

~ ~ ~

In this most favored month your celestial stars
And governing planet is Pluto. In most cases
This planet was known that is the coldest farthest
And isolated boldest in the solar system. Pluto has
Been known as the God of the underworld.
On another aspect of their personality is

The colorful floral flower is the Chrysanthemum.
This flower is also related to how a person
Born this month blossoms out to the freedom
Of how their environment and gaining an
Understanding of how their exterior complexities
Flourish and opens like the layers of the flower.

This shows and portrays their many elements
Of how others view their many joys on how
Their life unfolds into whatever they thrive to do.
Being a friend to them is knowing you'll have
a friend for life.
This gifted person born under this sign is
Known as one of the best true kind heart and
Loving gift within his or her mind.

~ ~ ~

Nov. 1

Their unto viewing a falling star
Lies straight ahead clear in sight
A knowledgeable noble man
Whom will acquire a well manner,
Of intelligence and make wise
Choices with all his thought.

Nov. 2

Contour to the thought that in this time of
Year there may be no snow at all.
Think twice before you tell tall tales
For in the end there may be a big snowfall.

Nov. 3

There in the far off distance into nearing
End of the autumn breezes may lie
A sleeping dog. Its master shall be
Calling him in to bed and does
Listen to this last night's call.

Nov. 4

In this time of year your noble mother
And father brought you into this world.
For many future years, they will always
Treasure your wee little toes and magical hands.
For they have known when they set their eyes
on you, that you'll always have
some form of creative
Hand, heart and soul.
Of wisest wisdom within your hearts voice.

Nov. 5

Listen to what nature is trying to tell you
Work its soil and you'll be granted with many
fields of feedings.
To keep your tummy well fed
with gracious natural elements.

Nov. 6

In this month of November there will be many
changes bestowed upon you.
Open your mind and you will know that
someone out there is certainly watching over you.

Nov. 7

May you never walk near a fountain of tears!
Be certain you'll look for a glowing element.
If you pick it up make sure you
pass it on to, one you love.
Then you'll be granted a willing
partner to have and to hold.

Nov. 8

On this day that you were born
Your sweet mother and father once
They set their eyes on you. They knew
that god had granted them a beauty of a
tender loving child with honesty granted.
In their little birth of this fine looking child.
Whether you were a little girl or boy
they will always know you'll be their
great treasures to their hearts.
Please know that you've held a nature
of humility and know that
You have a well refined mind and heart.

~ ~ ~

Sweet blessing to you will always
Be wrapped into your adoring eyes so true.
For within your sweet journey in life
You'll always be measured with
Your strong aptitude as you walk
In tune with all the powers within.
Your loving kind heart and knowledge
of a strong belief that you'll be coveted
by your ever-loving parents of love.

Nov. 9

Knowing ones destiny will be forever
Embedded within the farthest
Reaches of your enhancing heart.

Nov. 10

On this day that you were born
All the angels were playing songs
On their glorious harps of
Magical tunes with love and flair.
The cosmic stars are shining so bright
The angels are singing with all their might.
Just remember you have to make a firm
Commitment of treasures within
A timeless moment within the deepness
of your beloved heart.

Nov. 11

Throughout many years of long gone past
There will always be songs to be forever sang
To all that were lost in battles throw
Thus has not been forgotten as we all know
These songs will be sung forever in time

Of how all our long lost soldiers have
Gone and trembled in god's treasured
Heavenly arms of this I know.

~ ~ ~

One who was walking in and on this chosen path
Will always be measured as a well- defined man.
On their journeys home they may have
Taken the endless path to which
We'll all have to take on one's
Final destination.

~ ~ ~

Nov. 12

Dancing, frolicking throughout the lands
You'll always be singing in tune
with much in demand.
Your strong and vivid voice will be heard
As in time goes by every one will ever
tell you have a beautiful mind.

Nov. 13

In the meadow you will see the many wildflowers
How they all will sway in magical hues ray.

To be forever embedded upon our earth
May there always be a second birth.

Nov. 14

In all times off in the distant lands of valleys low
Walks many beauty of animals finding their
Way to the well forested lands and wanting
To bed down before the first fall of snow.

Nov. 15

I hear your whispers of undying love
This helps all make it through each day
The softness of your whispering song
Makes me want to travel to you today.

Nov. 16

May the bluebird of happiness never
Fly onto your nose, just let it flutter
By you with funnies as you go.

Nov. 17

In this merry month of November
There are so many pleasure's
you'll have to remember
Follow your heart and you'll have to treasure
The best things in life is your loving mother.

Nov. 18

On this beautiful day of so long ago
This day was brought forth
A beautiful child with beautiful glowing eyes
And sweet inviting smiles as one look
Could melt a mothers heart and soul;
As she held you in her arms
She had found that you
Gave her this beauty of
Sweetness into her
Loving eyes.

~ ~ ~

The best thing in life is making every moment
Count with great expectations is the
Beauty of you.

~ ~ ~

A timeless of treasures had entered your parents
Loving eyes as they enveloped you with
Their beauty of hearts; as they embraced you
Near their home of all living things will
Always be well remembered
Within their sweet memories.

~ ~ ~

On this day is your birthday, the element
Of your being as in the quality of water beneath
The surface and like the intellectual of the very
Essence in knowing you are aware of the intense
Look in your eyes is knowing that you're well
Loved by your partner, mother and other
Siblings was enveloped within your
True beauty of knowing that
Your well thought of
Through every day
And each year
There of.

~ ~ ~

This is the only month that has two different
Interplanetary ruling planets: the first planet is Pluto
Then after is the planet Mars, let
you be known your finest
Quality is the passions within your
hearts glow. When you
Make a friend, you make true friends,
for they shall be worthy

Of you in every step along the way.
Just keep your teasing at a low
level for sometimes caution will go
a long way. This month is
more favorable for you to look
for an ample destination
For carnal knowledge goes a long way for you.

Nov. 19

A wise man once said, don't let the little things
Bother you as you walk and enter through
A small opening of a door.

Nov. 20

There is a saying that whatever you know,
You may forget it if you don't write it down.
Just pick up a pencil or pen and make sure you put
it in a place you'll always remember.

Nov. 21

Magical moments don't happen everyday
Just look up into the rainbow hues
Then you'll remember the beauty upon you.

Nov. 23

Some of the good things in life,
Shouldn't have to cost a thousand dollars.
Look into your deep pockets for
Sometimes it could only cost one dollar
Or maybe even less.

Nov. 24

Cherish those moments that enter in your view
These sweet memories will be worth lasting.
In your well defined mind for an endless
gift of timeless inviting .
To the eternities of your educated
mind of longevity's rule.

Nov. 25

There's a feeling in the air with the light of a breeze
Can you feel the slight caress of
the last falling of leaves?
This magical feeling of all that
we know can be like an
intoxicating charismatic aura of autumnal scenic
songs of all that we know.

Nov. 26

Let there be no flow of teardrops tonight
For we all know there nearing is the
month of December will soon be here.
Make a wise decision to not spend
too much cash, for giving something
from the heart will be
loved from the bottom of their hearts.

Nov. 27

There is always an affordable solution to which
One can invest with an ample
amount of consideration.

Make the right move and all will be fortified
with one's reasoning upon one's mind.

Nov. 28

Never let anyone tell you to go buy some flowers
They may jump back at you and tell you
You really need to go and have a shower.

Nov. 29

The stillness of water, illustrates
a beauty of a reflection of a beautiful face.
Then as if a mirrored image thus lavished my eyes.
With the richness of your sweet smile ;
Has left me speechless of the beauty of you.

Nov. 30

The moral of the story is never let
A good man down for he'll always
Remember the image of your face.

~ ~ ~

The dawning of a new month ahead will bring
Peace and joy too many across the world.

Many people had been waiting
For an unknown child in Bethlehem
The sweetest baby divine may
Covet and adorn our earth
For he shall reign in all
Adulation of bringing
Peace and joy
To all shall live on in many people's minds
Throughout all the world with longevity
Living in the recesses of your mind.

~ ~ ~

In the joyous of the upcoming month ahead
There's a feeling in the air
That every child in any walk of life
Will soon be wishing that soon St. Nick will be here.

~ ~ ~

For onto the northern bright shiny star
There were many disciples walking to see
Within a manger laying in sweet Mary's arms.
Brought many happy cheer for
love and contentment .
She felt she brought a beautiful baby boy
into this world to become a
saviour to all among earth.

In all walks in time into which journey
All people on earth should have a divine
Purpose in life as they can be true to themselves
And own up their own values and beliefs.
Let there be known, don't ever envy your
friends or lovers or even your mothers.
For only you have one true mother which
Will always love you within her
last and final breath.

RUBY

December's Child

One may hold the key to which
You'll always be cherished near.
Your mother's loving eyes and
live with all the beauty of
what life has to offer you!
In this timely inspirational month
Of the whole year.

The element of your earnest heart
Is your fiery touch;
As for Jupiter
Is your glorifying planet all is
within your beautiful, optimistic heart.

In future years, your intellectual being will
be one of superior rational and insightful vision.

Upon your soul on the 20th of December
Is called the Peacock Ore.
The energy emanating from this resonates
A powerful energy crystal which you'll find
Too overcoming your indecisiveness.

December is the only month that
has three birthstones colors:
Turquoise, zircon, and tanzanite.

Dec. 1

In long and forgotten years, you may
Have been superficially related to
Mark Twain

Your most treasured element is your
Softness of strength which is quite intense
Within your very earnest soul.

Dec. 2

And onto the day that you were born
At that very first moment thus
The Holy Spirit had said, "I'll give you praise
Dear beloved father, sweet Lord of all on our heaven

and earth has been given to you
this beautiful child."
Blessed within all of the heavens above in your
Glorifying beloved hands.

~ ~ ~

For he who loves all throughout the many paths they
will walk in consternation with much fortitude.
Holding their loved one's hands invested
with the purity of love's white flying dove.

Dec. 3

There upon so many years ago was born
A true beauty which had an angelic smile
As she lays beside her mother's loving arms;
This mother was known as Mary Louise.
Which brought great joy to all her blessed
Children of long, long, ago with a wisdom
Far beyond her young years.
She'll always
Be known to me as a well cherished
Mother, a fine Christian woman with purity
in her whole inspiring loving heart.

~ ~ ~

Let there be known another baby was born
To which all of have known through out
Our hopes and dreams as she had chosen
The right path and made her dreams

A great living devotion and earning great
Skills as she walked the long endless path.
And now resides within our loving mothers arms
Into the heavens above, for she was my
Beloved sister Bernice Marie
Long may you rest in peace!

~ ~ ~

Dec. 4

There is a luminous glow as seen neath
The first fallen snow, it sparkles like
The stars in your eyes, when looking into them
Let all that you know, for you'll always be
Loved within our loving eyes as we do
see those sparkling loving eyes.

Dec. 5

There's a feeling in the air
That soon we'll be walking a well
Lighted path of snow and
Then we'll all have to
Bring out all the snow-shoveling tools.

Dec. 6

Once a upon a time of so long ago in the days
which had been born a child of this I surely know.
Was my beloved father which once
rode the rodeo Circuit.
This all happened before I was even born.
To me he was a good provider and always had
laughter in his eyes, his sense of
humor lives on inside of me.
He gave me his love of nature of
land and inviting laughter
into my heart. He long ago was to
meet my beautiful mom.
He truly adored her for she was
his divine precious love.

~ ~ ~

On this day that you were born
Your father led you into his well- trodden
Destination that he once walked before
The lavish green had been well-treated soil.
To embellish a spiritual healing force to
which you'll be teaching your children well.
For maybe they can become a healing soul.
To move ahead in times endless destination.
For onto each individual can keep our national
Native's history to live on with our grand-children
and great-grandchildren of how we came to be.

Dec. 7

If you were brought up in this time of year
Your earnest desires would become a
historical figure.
To which you'll leave a great legacy
for your many siblings more.

Dec. 8

This day brought forth a real
devotion throughout endless
times . Which all humanitarians of enlivened
qualities can bring and sing of beautiful things.

In every persons life there may be a peace offering
to adorn and adhere to what is known as
a self worth of an attitude
and forever keeping a straight forward
thought of being well preserved.

Dec. 9

There was a mother who brought forth
A son to which would lead his
children a legacy's worth to be

honest with whatever they want
to accomplish in life.
An equal amount of measure a fine statue of a man.
Just stand up for whatever you believe in your heart,
and never abuse the best thing in life.
For in his parting breath let my sons
be strong for what ever they want in life.
He was known in his past life as
a soldier like a Norseman
with the grace of Nobility as was
his father before him.

~ ~ ~

Make every moment count till you reach
Into the depth of your heart and be forever
loved till you find and reach with
your loving partners
love. A fine quality of life for the
rest of longevity's rule.

~ ~ ~

For fear not what has been given to you
Is the great love of all your children s precious,
Hearts of loving you for the man to which you are.

Dec. 10

I heard the calling of the owls upon this night
Their all whispering songs on to their mates.

For on this delightful night, their songs
Sure are a delight to hear for its
Song is like a soft feathered
Touch upon one's
Relaxing breath.

Dec. 11

In all honesty be truthful in this time
Of month; for this the season of
Showing off your sweet persona of tune.
Let all be known for tenderness at
This time of year, for all good people
on this gracious earth shall be in
Sweet rhapsodies tune.

Dec. 12

Can you feel my heart-beat?
To the rhythm of love's heat.
There's a true story told oh so long ago
These all- consuming moments
can make my heart glow
So listen to your heart and follow your dream.

Dec. 13

Unto a fortunate matter of many refined men
There will always be someone to love them.
With all their sweetest energies to which
Their beloved nature has honesty in their hearts.
Always remember there will be someone for you
If you keep your eyes wide-open
and let your heart glow.

Dec. 14

Onto another beauty of tune, let others
Enter and greet you with love and hope
of heart for its the season to reach out.
With human kindness and let others know
For you will reach a true kind heart with
Just a simple nod, with a smile upon
A fragile and timid mind.
Will be the best investment upon
one seeing a blessing in their mind.

Dec. 15

To love thy neighbor
Can make a big

Impression of a
Kind comment and be
in depth of all inviting concepts
Will go a long way in life.

Dec. 16

Tis the season to make some kind donation
To let others be happy upon this time of year.

~ ~ ~

On this day that you were born your
Mother will be your biggest and most inspirational
person in your young delightful life. Once she saw
your little eyes, she knew that someone was
watching over you.

Always know that your proud parents
Brought you into this world with sweet
love in both their eyes. You were once
chosen in your other forgotten life
of so many long and distant lands.
Of living in the past along with
The Disciples, when they all
followed the chosen child.

Dec. 17

Let there be peace and understanding
of knowing and
Giving to an understanding individual.
Will make a lasting impression
upon everyone's view.
At this time of year and knowing
You have done a good deed well done.

Dec. 18

In this merry month of December
There may be many sweet treasured
Happenings to all whom reaches
far beyond their ultimate powers.
For they have always been firm
believers in making every moment
count through each and everyday.
For now you'll always be a great leader
In all the things you say and do.

Dec. 19

Your pragmatic soul will always be
Kept at a distance with every decision

In your young life. While your reap your
mind and body just remember that you've
chosen the right path and destination.
For all your peers and family will always love
the gift of you and knowing your love too.

Dec. 20

On this magical day back in history
Just remember your proud parents
Brought home the best gift of all time.
Once they both looked into your eyes
They both knew that you'll be their
biggest star. That will live on in the depth
of their beautiful eyes. When God created
your whole being, he had enveloped
your shining beauty in every step and breath
of your beauty on your precious
face. In the highest peak in
the constellation, and throughout every
day in each and every step you take.

~ ~ ~

Always remember that everyone love's
the special young woman you've become,
Make every day a special moment.
You'll always be treasured in your loving
Mothers eyes through eternal
Kingdom's come.

Dec. 21

Upon this special day there had been
A chosen sun and chosen star
And bringing in a special
Little birth of a beautiful child
They brought you home
To their home sweet home.

Dec. 22

Christmas Blessings

Crimson thoughts can be full of beauty
Helpful and devotions can bring sweet purity
Rewards can we all enjoy this time of year merrily
Infinity throughout the past months so happily
So many songs are left to be sung with harmony
Too many people here on earth with love and gaiety
Music singing throughout this joyful year so freely
Announcing and listening to
angel voices sing sweetly
Saving, singing praises to all so
happy and lyrics beautifully.

Blessings to everyone at every
celebration at Christmas time

Long may everyone live in ever-
lasting harmonies rhyme
Enthusiastically singing praises of
love to everyone so divine
Soulful thoughts to one and all
each and every day in time
Secretly sanctifies beautiful minds to
all through each season so fine
Initiating God's love throughout every
thoughtful word will shine
Novel of words ingratiates great
tidings to all and all a
Good-night: may happiness reign in your life.

~ ~ ~

Dec. 23

Tis the season to know and keep
A well blessed thought to give and to
Hold from onto this beautiful time of
year that you'll always have a tremendous
Ever-lasting love to all mankind.
Know that you have the will to make
anyone's life well-nourished in all kinds of weather.
Whether it be cold, warm or an inviting calmness
Into your young heart.

Dec. 24

On this delightful day of so long ago
Your beautiful mother and father
Gave you the greatest gift of all.
The gift of life upon any given
day may you always remember
and cherish and love the
Beauty of your parents.
For you'll always have one true
loving parents to the end of time.
Making wise choices to make amends
For some day in the future they'll be laying
Beside our beautiful dear lord with all the beauty
Of all the loving Angels in glorious tune.
Through all loving hopes of sweet rhapsodies kiss.
God be with you in every step of the way.

Dec. 25

On this day that you were born the angels came
And brought forth a beautiful child all wrapped
Up with magical songs of joy in
their beauty of voice.
Always remember that there will always be
someone guiding through you all in life's journeys.
Through thick and sometimes thin but remember
on this day only think of magical songs and

the joys of your loving one's dearest thoughts.
In everything you say and do; for in all the days
and upcoming New Year.
We are all sending you the most greatest gift
of all our magical thoughts delight.
For all eternity and time
Let there be peace
On earth to all
The beautiful
People to
Which
Can bring joy to one
and all of the days ahead.
We'll be sending merry Christmas to everyone
And to many A happy good night of treasures
and sweet dreams ahead.

Dec. 26

Let us all go sledding, skating, caroling, singing
And sing sweet music to one and all.
For we'll be treasuring to make the
remaining of the year a memorable one as we
anticipate a New Year is almost
upon this time of year.
Make no mistake there is a
feeling in the air that no one can deny.
We'd all be quite merry in showing all
our beloved gifts to one and another

171

for its the season to be filled with
the beautiful star and dancing
Moon above. Just keep in the
deepest part of your gracious
And beautiful mind and
Wish peace on earth
To last for eternal
Love of flame.
Amen.

~ ~ ~

Dec. 27

Be fruitful as you walk in
contemplating your next move
For the epitome of you is like a rolling gift of love
Which then you'll become like the gift of greatness
Like the all elusive stars all glittering above.

Dec. 28

Let there be no stone left in your path
For all your purposes will be met by a force
To be reckoned with into your journeys:
And path in life as while you'll be walking
along with your best of friends.

Dec. 29

In the coming months ahead, there may be
three different paths that you'll have to cross,
Make the wise choice for going on the wrong
One might lead to you meeting someone
Who'll lead you a stray!!!

~ ~ ~

In this precious time of the year
There will a big decision you'll have to make
Let no one steer you into a clearance you know
Nothing about, just relax a while and contemplate
Of how you'll make the right choice of matters
To which you'll be reflective in all that means;
Most to you as you walk underneath that
Beautiful rainbow of breath's request.

Dec. 30

In all the world there will be many people that
You'll meet up with, make sure you
open your mind and heart.
For clearly this may be the best
that life has to offer you,
in your destined chosen path.
In everything that you love and cherish in life there

Eve Theresa Marie Carter

Is and always will be like your
greatest gift of stardom
Thus within the beauty of your
loving partners eyes and soul.

Dec. 31

On this blessed day an angel brought your proud
Parents a child to cherish in everyday
forward from this time on.
For he gave you the best thing that one
man or woman can ever want.
A sweet bundle of joy for all to be
seen through all the days ahead.
A beautiful bouncing boy filled with a
love that no one could ever imagine.
One look at your angel like face brought
many tears of happy fulfilling love.
To live forever in your little heart
as if it was touched by
A beloved angel on wings.

May you forever be embedded with
sparkles in your life and eyes!
As you walk into the valley of what is really you.

Printed in the United States
By Bookmasters